This Book is presented to:

<u>Evan's Mommy</u>

_____

By:

<u>Christ The King</u>

<u>Nursery School</u>

This edition published 2008 by Concordia Publishing House
3558 S. Jefferson Avenue, St. Louis, MO 63118-3968
1-800-325-3040 • www.cph.org

Text copyright © 2006 by Julie Stiegemeyer
Illustrations copyright © 2006 by Concordia Publishing House
Cover and interior fabric design © Coventry Cottage by Linda Hohag

Scripture quotations are from The Holy Bible, English Standard Version. Copyright © 2001 by Crossway Bibles,
a publishing ministry of Good News Publishers, Wheaton, Illinois. Used by permission. All rights reserved.

Manufactured in China

1   2   3   4   5   6   7   8   9   10   17   16   15   14   13   12   11   10   09   08

Mommy Promises

By JULIE STIEGEMEYER

Illustrated by WILSON ONG

CONCORDIA PUBLISHING HOUSE • SAINT LOUIS

For my own mom,
whose love and support
has taught me about helping others
and keeping promises. —J.S.

For weeks and months, you grew and grew
as we prepared for you to join our family.

When you arrived, we learned to care for you.
I marveled at your tiny fingers and toes. I watched
you sleep and memorized the curves of your face.

And I made promises I'm still learning to keep.

Foreword

I will gather you in my arms and wrap

you in warmth and love, just like

Mary held her infant Jesus.

For a time, God gave me your hands to

hold, your tears to dry, your cheeks

to kiss—God made you my child.

Even better, God adopts you as His

own in Baptism. He forgives your sins.

Now you are a child of God.

I will teach you to sing like angels

about glad tidings for a Savior born

among us, and I'll tell you about

His redeeming death and an Easter

resurrection. **I promise.**

I will give you the things you need:

a warm coat for snowy days, a soft bed for

quiet nights, and your fuzzy blankey too.

I will scrub-a-dub you with bubbles

and let you play in the bath until

your fingertips are raisins.

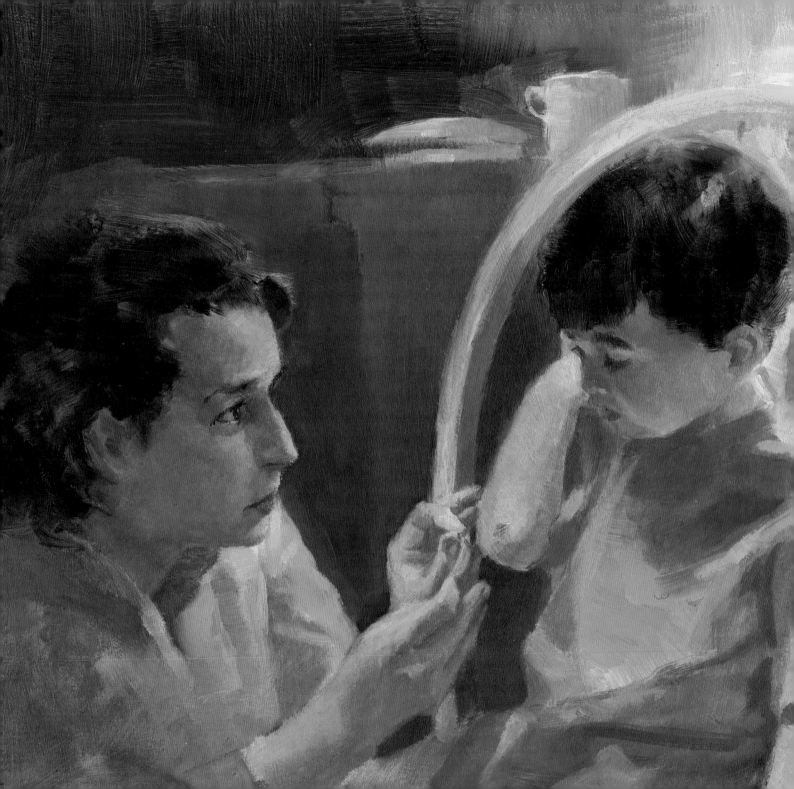

I will hold your hand when we cross the street,

and help you learn that obeying your parents keeps you safe.

But I'll also let you learn to climb trees, although you might fall.

I'll be ready with hugs and Band-Aids.

I will take time to listen—from your first words to your curious questions. And I'll do my best to answer why cats have whiskers and where the wind comes from.

I'll read you stories about foxes and crows, dogs

and their bones. We'll read about quests and kings,

children and a wardrobe. And I'll keep reading

to you even after you read on your own.

We'll also read about how God split a sea in two,

saved a man from lions, and made the blind see.

In story after story, we'll learn about how God

always keeps His promises. Every one.

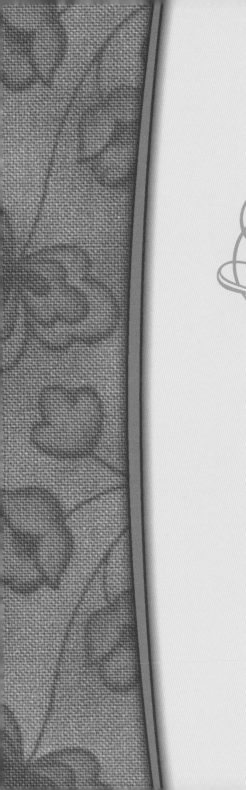

I'll help you learn to help yourself:

to brush your own teeth,

to tie your own shoes,

and to read your own books.

I promise.

I will give you all the foods that make you grow—

chicken and carrots, cantaloupe and tomatoes from the

farmers market. And we'll also make your favorite cookies

often—peanut butter chocolate chip.

Together, we will give thanks for our food and all

of God's gifts—even on tuna casserole night.

I will help you study your spelling words
and multiplication tables.

I'll also teach you that wisdom begins with
God's grace and knowing Jesus, our Savior.

I will reassure you that you are never alone—even
when shadows lurk in the corners of your bedroom.

We will pray together and remember that God's
angels guard us all through the night.

I promise.

 I will cheer you on from the sidelines, even when the game isn't going well. We'll talk about trying even when it's hard, being a friend to players who struggle, and showing grace in wins and losses.

Just like you, I'm still learning to listen

better, to pray even when I'm tired,

to be more patient. Only God is perfect,

so we'll ask for forgiveness together.

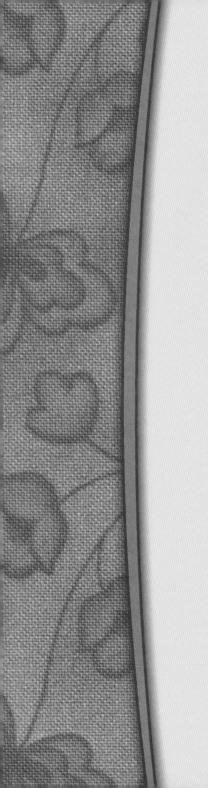

From your first steps to your first home run,

from your first day of school to your graduation,

and from your first breath to your last, your heavenly

Father will care for you.

And I will love you all along the way.

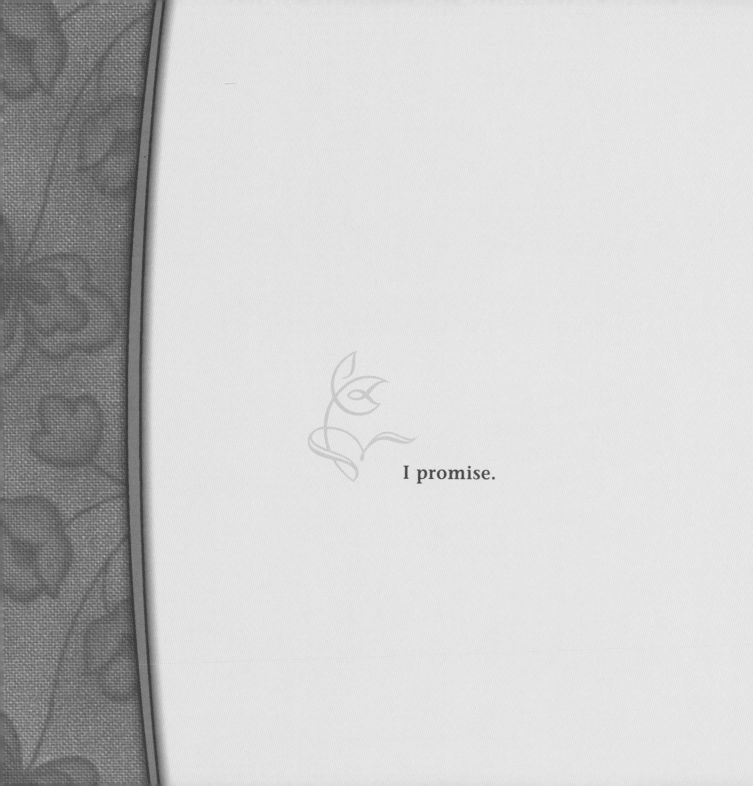

I promise.

Julie Stiegemeyer is the author of several books, including Saint Nicholas: The Real Story of the Christmas Legend, Thanksgiving: A Harvest Celebration, and Bright Easter Day. *Julie also enjoys teaching music to children at her church. She was born in Denver, Colorado, but now makes her home in Fort Wayne, Indiana, with her husband, Scott, and son, Jacob.*

Wilson Ong was born and raised near San Francisco, California. After attending the Arts Students' League in New York, he embarked on a professional career of painting and illustrating, garnering various national awards. Mr. Ong also spent nine years as an art teacher. His wife, Kathy, and their four daughters have often been counted on as inspiration to his artwork.